ABG Practice Questions

35 Practice Questions, Answers, and Rationales on Arterial Blood Gases

By Johnny Lung RRT

Disclaimer:

Medicine and respiratory therapy are continuously changing practices. The author and publisher have reviewed all information in this report with resources believed to be reliable and accurate and have made every effort to provide information that is up to date with the best practices at the time of publication. Despite our best efforts we cannot disregard the possibility of human error and continual changes in best practices the author, publisher, and any other party involved in the production of this work can warrant that the information contained herein is complete or fully accurate. The author, publisher, and all other parties involved in this work disclaim all responsibility from any errors contained within this work and from the results from the use of this information. Readers are encouraged to check all information in this book with institutional guidelines, other sources, and up to date information. Respiratory Therapy Zone is not affiliated with the NBRC, AARC, or any other group at the time of this publication.

Copyright © Respiratory Therapy Zone

Table of Contents

INTRODUCTION..4

SECTION 1 6

SECTION 2 55

CONCLUSION...91

REFERENCES 94

Introduction

Are you preparing to take the TMC Exam? Or do you just need some extra practice when it comes to learning about Arterial Blood Gases? If so, then this is the right book for you.

In the coming pages, you will find 35 practice questions in the exact format of the ones you'll see on the actual TMC Exam, all covering the topic of ABGs. Each question contains the correct answer, along with a detailed rationale explaining why that answer is correct.

Arterial Blood Gas analysis is one of the most important sections of the TMC Exam. With that being said, this information definitely is not easy for most students.

This is not a reason to panic!

It just means that you should certainly invest a lot of your time learning concepts of ABGs. The good thing is, the practice questions in this book can help you do just that.

This book is broken up into two sections.

Section 1 is for practicing. It includes the question, answer, and rationale all on the same page, for an easy-to-read and learn review.

Section 2 is for testing. It contains the same questions, however, the answer is no longer given. This way, you can quiz yourself to see what you've learned. This is great for practicing while on the go, because you can highlight using the Kindle app. Then, you'll be able to go back and see which questions you answered incorrectly.

Are you ready to take your knowledge of Arterial Blood Gases to the next level and prepare to pass the TMC Exam on your very next attempt? If so, let's go ahead and dive right in!

Section 1
(Practice Mode)

1. An adult patient with shortness of breath is admitted to the emergency department. An ABG has been collected and shows the following results:
   pH 7.51
   PaCO2 26 torr
   PaO2 57 torr
   HCO3- 24 mEq/L
   Which of the following best describes the patient's status?
   A. The patient has a metabolic issue
   B. The patient is hypoventilating
   C. The primary concern is hypoxemia
   D. The patient is in impending respiratory failure

The first thing we must do with this question is interpret the ABG results. By doing so, we see that the patient is in acute respiratory alkalosis due to hyperventilation.

So we can immediately see that the patient is not hypoventilating, nor are they in impending respiratory failure. Also, we already determined that there is a respiratory issue, not a metabolic issue, so we can rule that one out as well.

Since the PaO2 is below 60, this means that the patient is hypoxemic, so their oxygenation status is our primary concern. It's what's causing the patient to hyperventilate and feel shortness of breath.

So by using what we know about ABG interpretation, as well as the process of elimination, we can determine that the correct answer has to be C.

The correct answer is: C. The primary concern is hypoxemia

2. The physician put in an order for an ABG that was not STAT. You weren't busy so you went ahead and collected the sample. What is the best way to avoid analysis errors associated with running the sample?
   A. Analyze the sample immediately
   B. Place the sample in an ice slush
   C. Use dry instead or liquid heparin
   D. Uncap the syringe to remove any air

The most common cause of errors when running an ABG sample has to do with the time removed and temperature of the sample.

In a perfect world, all ABG samples should be analyzed immediately. If the sample cannot be analyzed within 15 minutes, it should be placed in an ice slush.

So by using what we know about ABG analysis, we can determine that the correct answer has to be A.

The correct answer is: A. Analyze the sample immediately

3. The physician ordered an ABG on a 41-year-old patient with COPD. Before drawing the sample from the radial artery, which of the following should be performed?
   A. Check the patient's oxygen saturation
   B. Modified Allen test
   C. Nail bed blanching
   D. Blood pressure measurement

ALWAYS remember— whenever you're going to stick an ABG in the radial artery, you first have to perform the modified Allen test in order to check for collateral circulation.

The test is performed by occluding the radial artery to check for circulation through the ulnar artery. That way, if something happens to the radial artery during an ABG stick, the hand will still be perfused via the ulnar artery.

None of the other answer choices are required before an ABG stick, so we know that the correct answer has to be B.

The correct answer is: B. Modified Allen test

4. A 48-year-old female patient has been admitted to the emergency department with the following arterial blood gas results:
   pH 7.54
   PaCO2 29 torr
   PaO2 86 torr
   HCO3- 24 mEq/L
   Which of the following is the best interpretation of these results?
   A. Metabolic acidosis
   B. Metabolic alkalosis
   C. Respiratory acidosis
   D. Respiratory alkalosis

This is just a classic ABG interpretation question. You likely won't see many of these on the TMC Exam because at this point, the NBRC will assume that you already know how to interpret ABGs. Otherwise, you wouldn't have made it this far.

With that said, you still absolutely MUST know how to interpret them because you will be required to do so for SEVERAL questions on the exam.

So now let's go ahead and interpret this one. The pH is increased, which means alkalosis. The PaCO2 is decreased and the bicarbonate level is normal. That means that the interpretation is acute respiratory alkalosis with normal oxygenation. The correct answer is D.

The correct answer is: D. Respiratory alkalosis.

5. You are needed to help with the treatment of a patient with pneumonia that is receiving oxygen via nasal cannula at 4 L/min. The physician asks for your suggestion of the best way to evaluate the patient's overall ability to breathe. What should you recommend?
   A. Performing pulse oximetry
   B. Drawing an arterial blood sample for analysis
   C. Performing a forced vital capacity measurement
   D. Doing a full set of pulmonary function tests

To get this one right, you simply just had to have a basic understanding of the purpose drawing an ABG. The results of an ABG can help us assess the patient's ability to oxygenate and ventilate—meaning that it assesses their ability to breathe.

Pulse oximetry only assesses the patient's oxygenation status—not the ventilation status. PFTs do not give any information on the PaO2 or PaCO2 levels, so we can rule out C and D as well.

So by using what we know about ABGs, as well as the process of elimination, you know that the correct answer has to be B.

The correct answer is: B. Drawing an arterial blood sample for analysis

6. A 56-year-old male patient's status has gotten worse over the past 2 hours. He went from an air entrainment mask to a nonrebreather, and is now receiving positive pressure ventilation with the following settings:
   Assist control rate of 12
   Tidal volume 650 mL
   FIO2 100%
   PIP 40 cm H2O
   Plateau pressure 35 cm H2
   The patient's arterial blood gas results are as follows:
   pH 7.42
   PaCO2 35 torr
   PaO2 54 torr
   SpO2 84%
   HCO3- 23 mEq/L
   Which of the following best represents the status of this patient?
   A. Cystic fibrosis
   B. Acute metabolic alkalosis
   C. Hypoventilation from fatigue
   D. A significant intrapulmonary shunt

The ventilator settings appear to be set properly because the ABG results tell us that the patient's ventilatory status is good, being that the pH and PaCO2 are in the normal ranges. This issue here is with the patient's oxygenation.

The PaO2 and SpO2 are extremely low, especially considering that the patient is receiving an FiO2 of 100%. This is a classic case of refractory hypoxemia that is most likely caused by intrapulmonary shunting.

We know that this is the case because the patient is not responding to high levels of oxygen. The patient needs PEEP in this case.

So by using what we know about intrapulmonary shunting, we can determine that the correct answer has to be D.

The correct answer is: D. A significant intrapulmonary shunt

7. A 60-year-old female patient has been admitted to the emergency department with the following ABG results:
   pH 7.48
   PaCO2 41 torr
   PaO2 98 torr
   HCO3- 52 mEq/L
   These results of this ABG can be interpreted as:
   A. Respiratory alkalosis
   B. Respiratory acidosis
   C. Metabolic alkalosis
   D. Metabolic acidosis

This is just a classic ABG interpretation question. You likely won't see many of these on the TMC Exam because at this point, the NBRC will assume that you already know how to interpret ABGs. Otherwise, you wouldn't have made it this far.

With that said, you still absolutely MUST know how to interpret them because you will be required to do so for SEVERAL questions on the exam.

So let's go ahead and break this one down. The pH is increased which means that alkalosis is present. The PaCO2 is in the normal range and the bicarb level is increased. So this ABG can be interpreted as metabolic alkalosis, which means that the correct answer is C.

The correct answer is: C. Metabolic alkalosis

8. An ABG is drawn on 71-year-old patient with a history of chronic COPD. After reviewing the patient's ABG results, which of the following values would be most reflective of the severity of the patient's chronic condition?
   A. pH
   B. PaCO2
   C. HCO3-
   D. PaO2

This one is a little tricky. Since the question tells us that the patient has chronic COPD, that means that they are a CO2 retainer. So with that said, we should expect their PaCO2 levels to be increased.

So in this case, the arterial Bicarb level is actually most reflective of chronic CO2 retention. With an increased PaCO2, the body will compensate by increasing the amount of Bicarb in order to get the pH back into the normal range.

The pH, PaCO2, and PaO2 values tell us more about the patient's acute condition — whereas the question is asking about the patient's chronic condition. So now we know that the correct answer has to be C.

The correct answer is: C. HCO3-

9. A patient has been admitted to the emergency department with the following arterial blood gas results:
   pH 7.24
   PaCO2 29 torr
   PaO2 81 torr
   HCO3- 13 mEq/L
   Which of the following best describes the given results?
   A. Partially compensated metabolic alkalosis
   B. Partially compensated metabolic acidosis
   C. Uncompensated respiratory acidosis
   D. Uncompensated respiratory alkalosis

This is just a classic ABG interpretation question. You likely won't see many of these on the TMC Exam because at this point, the NBRC will assume that you already know how to interpret ABGs. Otherwise, you wouldn't have made it this far.

With that said, you still absolutely MUST know how to interpret them because you will be required to do so for SEVERAL questions on the exam.

So now let's go ahead and interpret this one. The pH is decreased which means acidosis. The Bicarb is severely low which tells us that there is a metabolic issue. The PaCO2 is also low, because in this case, the body is hyperventilating to try to blow off some CO2 in order to bring the pH back up into the normal range.

However, it has not compensated enough to fully bring the pH into the normal range, so we know that it is only partially compensated. That means that the correct answer is B.

The correct answer is: B. Partially compensated metabolic acidosis

10. The following ABG results were obtained on a 54-year-old female patient that is breathing room air:
    pH 7.30
    PaCO2 57 torr
    PaO2 61 torr
    HCO3- 24 mEq/L
    Which of the following best describes the given results?
    A. Normal blood gas with mild hypoxemia
    B. Fully compensated metabolic acidosis with mild hypoxemia
    C. Acute respiratory alkalosis with mild hypoxemia
    D. Acute uncompensated respiratory acidosis with mild hypoxemia

This is just a classic ABG interpretation question. You likely won't see many of these on the TMC Exam because at this point, the NBRC will assume that you already know how to interpret ABGs. Otherwise, you wouldn't have made it this far.

With that said, you still absolutely MUST know how to interpret them because you will be required to do so for SEVERAL questions on the exam.

So now let's interpret this one.

The pH decreased which means acidosis. The PaCO2 is increased and the Bicarb is in the normal range. This tells us that there respiratory acidosis with no compensation because the Bicarb is normal. The PaO2 is decreased as well, which tells us that there is hypoxemia. So we know that the correct answer is D.

The correct answer is: D. Acute uncompensated respiratory acidosis with mild hypoxemia

11. A patient with acute respiratory acidosis would be expected to have a base excess in the range of which of the following?
    A. + 6 mEq/L
    B. - 6 mEq/L
    C. +/- 2 mEq/L
    D. +/- 8 mEq/L

To get this one right, you simply just had to know the normal range for Base Excess—which of course, is +/- 2 mEq/L.

Base Excess simply refers to the excess amount of base that's present in the blood.

The question tells us that the patient has acute or uncompensated respiratory acidosis, and in this case, the base excess should always fall within the normal range.

In another scenario, if there was renal compensation present, like you would see in a patient with chronic COPD, the Base Excess would be elevated above the normal range due to the increased levels of Bicarb. Remember, when the PaCO2 levels are chronically increased, the Bicarb levels will increase as well in order to compensate.

But for this patient, there is an acute condition so we know that the correct answer has to be C.

The correct answer is: C. +/- 2 mEq/L

12. Which of the following ABG results would you most likely see for a patient who is having a mild asthma attack?
    A. pH = 7.30 PaCO2 = 49 torr PaO2 = 61 torr
    B. pH = 7.41 PaCO2 = 51 torr PaO2 = 51 torr
    C. pH = 7.45 PaCO2 = 42 torr PaO2 = 52 torr
    D. pH = 7.47 PaCO2 = 30 torr PaO2 = 62 torr

To get this one right, you have to be familiar with the typical ABG results that you would see for a patient with asthma.

For a mild asthma attack, you would expect the results to show respiratory alkalosis with hypoxemia. That is because, for a mild attack, it's normal for the patient to be hyperventilating due to the shortness of breath. Now we just have to go through the answer choices to find the set of results for this interpretation.

We can automatically rule out A because the pH is decreased, which means acidosis is present. B and C both show alkalosis, however, in both cases the PaCO2 is elevated which means that it's a metabolic issue—not respiratory alkalosis. So we can rule out those two as well.

For option D, the pH is increased and the PaCO2 is decreased, which shows respiratory alkalosis. Also note that the PaO2 is decreased, which indicates that hypoxemia is present. That means that we now know that the correct answer has to be D.

The correct answer is: D. pH = 7.47 PCO2 = 30 torr PaO2 = 62 torr

13. The following ABG results were obtained on a 28-year-old female patient:
    pH 7.28
    PaCO2 22 torr
    HCO3 12 mEq/L
    BE -13
    PaO2 111 torr
    Her ABG results indicate which of the following?
    A. Acute metabolic alkalosis
    B. Partially compensated metabolic acidosis
    C. Partially compensated respiratory alkalosis
    D. Acute respiratory acidosis

This is just a classic ABG interpretation question. You likely won't see many of these on the TMC Exam because at this point, the NBRC will assume that you already know how to interpret ABGs. Otherwise, you wouldn't have made it this far.

With that said, you still absolutely MUST know how to interpret them because you will be required to do so for SEVERAL questions on the exam.

So now let's go ahead and interpret this one. The pH is decreased which means acidosis. The Bicarb and Base Excess levels are severely decreased, which tells us that there is a metabolic issue. The low PaCO2 tells us that the patient is trying to compensate by hyperventilating, but since the pH is still outside of the normal range, there is only partial compensation.

So we know that the correct answer has to be B.

The correct answer is: B. Partially compensated metabolic acidosis

14. A 61-year-old female patient with a history of COPD was admitted to the emergency department for an acute case suspected pneumonia. Her ABG results are as follows:
   pH = 7.19
   PCO2 = 66 torr
   HCO3 = 26 mEq/L
   PaO2 = 41 torr
   P(A-a)O2 = 43 torr
   Which of the following best describes the patient's condition?
   A. Acute hypercapnic respiratory failure
   B. Chronic hypercapnic respiratory failure
   C. Acute hypoxemic respiratory failure
   D. Combined hypercapnic and hypoxemic respiratory failure

Let's break this one down.

Right away, you should notice that the patient's oxygenation values are severely low. The pH is decreased and the PaCO2 is increased, which means acidosis—and in this case—respiratory failure.

In this patient's case, the patient is in respiratory failure not only due to ventilatory issues, but also for oxygenation issues as well. In other words, her ABG results show hypercapnia (increased PaCO2) and hypoxemia (decreased PaO2), so we know that the correct answer has to be D.

The correct answer is: D. Combined hypercapnic and hypoxemic respiratory failure

15. A 48-year-old male patient is receiving volume-control SIMV with 40% oxygen and has following ABG results:
    pH 7.51
    PaCO2 27 torr
    PaO2 85 torr
    HCO3 24 mEq/L
    BE -1
    The patient's blood gas results indicate which of the following?
    A. Acute respiratory alkalosis
    B. Acute respiratory acidosis
    C. Acute metabolic alkalosis
    D. Acute hypoxemic failure

To get this one right, you have to be able to interpret the ABG results. Let's break this one down.

The pH is increased which means alkalosis. The Bicarb and Base Excess values are in the normal range and the PaCO2 is decreased. This tells us that there is respiratory acidosis.

There is no compensation going on here, since the Bicarb level is normal and the pH is outside of the normal range. Also note, the oxygenation status is normal as well, which we know this because the PaO2 is normal.

The results show uncompensated respiratory alkalosis, so we know that the correct answer has to be A.

The correct answer is: A. Acute respiratory alkalosis

16. Which of the following problems is most likely associated with a patient whose ABG results show respiratory alkalosis?
   A. Hypoxemia
   B. Hypothermia
   C. CNS depression
   D. Opiate overdose

To get this one right, you had to know the cause of respiratory alkalosis. Also, of course, you had to know that respiratory alkalosis is often a side effect of hypoxemia.

When a patient has decreased oxygen levels, they will hyperventilate which is what causes the respiratory alkalosis ABG results. Remember, hyperventilation decreases the PaCO2 values.

None of the other answer choices make sense in this situation, so we know that the correct answer has to be A.

The correct answer is: A. Hypoxemia

17. A 54-year-old female patient on the general floor has the following ABG results:
    pH = 7.53
    pCO2 = 44 torr
    HCO3 = 34 mEq/L
    Which of the following is the best interpretation of these results?
    A. Acute respiratory alkalosis
    B. Acute metabolic alkalosis
    C. Compensated respiratory alkalosis
    D. Combined respiratory and metabolic alkalosis

This is your typical ABG interpretation question. Let's break this one down.

The pH is elevated which means alkalosis. The PaCO2 is in the normal range. The Bicarb is elevated, which tells us that there is a metabolic issue. And since we already determined that the pH is elevated and the PaCO2 is normal, there is no compensation going on here.

So that rules out all of the other answer choices and we know that the correct answer has to be B.

The correct answer is: B. Acute metabolic alkalosis

18. While interpreting a patient's ABG results, you note a PaCO2 of 24 torr, a Base Excess of -11 mEq/L, and a pH of 7.36. How would you interpret these results?
    A. Acute respiratory alkalosis
    B. Acute metabolic acidosis
    C. Compensated respiratory alkalosis
    D. Compensated metabolic acidosis

This is your typical ABG interpretation question. Let's break this one down.

The pH is in the normal range. The PaCO2 is decreased, and the Base Excess is decreased. When you have abnormal values but yet a normal pH, this tells us immediately that there is come compensation going on.

The pH is on the low end of the normal range, meaning that it is less than 7.40. This tells us that the primary problem is acidosis. And since the Base Excess is severely low, we know that there is a metabolic issue. The PaCO2 is also low because the body is compensating for the low Base Excess in order to bring the pH back into the normal range.

So now we know that the correct answer has to be D.

The correct answer is: D. Compensated metabolic acidosis

19. A 69-year-old male patient in the ICU displays the following ABG results:
    pH = 7.43
    pCO2 = 21 torr
    HCO3 = 13 mEq/L
    His ABG results can be interpreted as which of the following?
    A. Acute respiratory alkalosis
    B. Partially compensated respiratory alkalosis
    C. Fully compensated respiratory alkalosis
    D. Combined respiratory and metabolic alkalosis

This is your typical ABG interpretation question. Let's break this one down.

The pH is in the normal range. The PaCO2 is decreased which tells us that the patient is hyperventilating. The Bicarb is decreased.

The pH is on the high end of the normal range, meaning that it is greater than 7.40. This tells us that the primary problem is alkalosis. And since the PaCO2 is severely low, we know that there is a respiratory issue because the patient is hyperventilating.

The Bicarb is also low because the body is compensating for the hyperventilation in order to bring the pH back into the normal range. So now we know that the correct answer has to be C.

The correct answer is: C. Fully compensated respiratory alkalosis

20. A patient's ABG results show that she has a pH of 7.56 and a PaCO2 of 48 torr. Based on the results given, how would you interpret the patient's status?
    A. Respiratory alkalosis
    B. Respiratory acidosis
    C. Metabolic acidosis
    D. Metabolic alkalosis

For this ABG interpretation question, they only give you two of the ABG values, so you have to use some critical thinking in order to figure this one out.

The pH is high, which indicates alkalosis. So with that, we can already rule out the answer choices containing acidosis.

Next, we can see that the PaCO2 is elevated. When there is a high pH, we know that the only two possible causes could be either respiratory alkalosis or metabolic alkalosis. And in this case, the pH is increased which means that it can't be respiratory alkalosis.

So by using our illustrious ABG interpretation skills, as well as the process of elimination, we know that the correct answer has to be D.

The correct answer is: D. Metabolic alkalosis

21. You were just called by the physician for a STAT ABG. Before entering the patient's room, you must first gather all the necessary supplies. Which of the following is required in order to perform an arterial puncture?
    A. Sterile gloves
    B. Lancet
    C. Local anesthetic
    D. Anticoagulant

To get this one right, you have to know what supplies are REQUIRED in order to collect an ABG sample. The key word here is: required.

You are required to use the following equipment: syringe, anticoagulant, transport container with label, for example, a biohazard bag. Keep in mind, you will also need a container with ice if you are unable to analyze the sample immediately. You also need antiseptic swabs, tape or a bandage, clean exam gloves, and sterile gauze.

A local anesthetic is not required— it is optional. A lancet is used for capillary sampling—not for an arterial puncture. And yes, you must wear gloves when sticking an ABG, but they do not have to be <u>sterile</u> gloves.

So by using what we know about collecting an ABG, as well as the process of elimination, we know that the correct answer has to be D.

The correct answer is: D. Anticoagulant

22. There is an order to obtain a blood sample from a neonate. It is determined that you should obtain the sample from a capillary instead of the artery. Which of the following is true regarding a capillary blood gas sample?
    A. To obtain the sample, you need to milk the puncture site
    B. The sample must be drawn from the first drop of surface blood
    C. The pH and PCO2 correlate well with arterial blood
    D. The puncture normally is performed on the ball of the foot

You must be familiar with the heel-stick procedure in infants in order to get this one correct.

The lateral aspect of the heel is the most common site for collecting a capillary blood sample in infants. After you puncture the infant's heel, you should wipe away first drop of blood and observe for free flow before collection. You do not need to squeeze the heel.

Because the infant's arteries are so tiny, it's very difficult to stick them with a needle. So that is why we use capillary blood from the heel instead. But there are some differences in the ABG values of capillary blood when compared to arterial blood. And you must know these difference for the TMC Exam.

Capillary blood correlates well with the pH and PaCO2 values of arterial blood. Therefore, it is useful ONLY for assessing the acid-base status.

Capillary blood does not correlate well with the PaO2 values, so you should never use a capillary sample to assess the infant's oxygenation status. So after going through all the answer choices, we can determine that the correct answer has to be C.

The correct answer is: C. The pH and PCO2 correlate well with arterial blood

23. Which of the following infection control procedures is to be used when drawing an arterial blood gas?
    A. Hand washing and gloves only
    B. Gown and protective eyewear
    C. Mask and protective eyewear
    D. All CDC standard precautions

You should be able to select the correct answer for this one quick and easily.

You should always use ALL CDC standard precautions for any patient in every scenario– including, of course, drawing an ABG.

You must always wash your hands and wear gloves, as well as wear the appropriate masks, gowns, and eyewear when necessary. That means that the correct answer has to be D.

The correct answer is: D. All CDC standard precautions

24. After collecting an ABG sample, you are about the analyze the sample using a point-of-care analyzer. During the process, the device flags the PaCO2 results. Which of the following should you do at this time?
   A. Send the sample to the central lab for analysis
   B. Repeat the analysis using a fresh sample and the same cartridge
   C. Repeat analysis using a fresh sample and new cartridge
   D. Repeat the analysis using the same sample and same cartridge

When using a point-of-care analyzer, sometimes it will flag the sample. When this occurs, it usually means that one of the values is outside the analyzer's reportable range.

So in this case, you should send the sample to the central lab for analysis. They will be able to analyze to sample properly and give you accurate results so that you can proceed to treat the patient.

None of the other answer choices really make sense in this situation, so we know that the correct answer has to be A.

The correct answer is: A. Send the sample to the central lab for analysis

25. A patient in the emergency department is receiving oxygen via a nonrebreather at 15 L/min. There ABG results are as follows:
pH 7.21
PaCO2 38 torr
PaO2 569 torr
SpO2 100%
HCO3 23 mEq/L
BE -1
Which of the following is the best interpretation for these results?
A. Respiratory acidosis
B. Metabolic acidosis
C. Laboratory error
D. Large physiologic shunt

This appears to be a typical ABG interpretation question, but after looking at the results, one major value should stand out like a sore thumb.

Before you even attempt to interpret the acid-base status, you should automatically know that a PaO2 of 569 torr on 100% oxygen is not only possible.

The PaCO2 and the Bicarb values are both in the normal ranges. That means that the pH should be normal as well, but it's not— it's decreased.

So taking everything into consideration, you know that the only possibility here is a laboratory error. The correct answer has to be C.

The correct answer is: C. Laboratory error

26. A 51-year-old patient on room air has the following ABG results:
    pH 7.43
    PaCO2 47 torr
    PaO2 169 torr
    Which of the following is the best action to take?
    A. Report the results to the attending physician
    B. Report the results to the patient's nurse
    C. Discard the sample and obtain a new one
    D. Give the patient a bronchodilator treatment

To get this one correct, there is a very important detail in the question that you needed to notice, and it is: The patient is breathing room air!

Now, when you look at their results, you should know that a PaO2 above 120 torr is not possible for a patient that is only breathing room air. This would require that the patient is receiving some type of supplemental oxygen. So you know that there is an error with the sample.

In the case, you wouldn't want to report these erroneous results and there is no indication for a bronchodilator at this time. So now you know that the correct answer has to be C.

The correct answer is: C. Discard the sample and obtain a new one

27. A patient with a flail chest arrives to the emergency department and is hyperventilating. Which of the following ABG results would you expect to find for this patient?
    A. Increased pH and decreased SaO2
    B. Increased pH and increased SaO2
    C. Decreased pH and decreased SaO2
    D. Decreased pH and increased SaO2

First and foremost, the question tells us that the patient is hyperventilating, which means that they are blowing off too much CO2. With that said, you should automatically know that the pH will be increased.

And for a patient with a flail chest, you would expect them to have hypoxemia as well.

So by breaking this one down, you should be able to easily determine that the correct answer is A.

The correct answer is: A. Increased pH and decreased SaO2

28. After drawing an ABG sample, you notice that the blood appears to be darker in color. You suspect that obtained sample is actually venous blood. Which of the following would be the best way to confirm this suspicion?
    A. Get a second opinion from the attending physician
    B. Compute the alveolar-arterial O2 gradient
    C. Compute the patient's P/F ratio
    D. Cross-check the results against the patient's SpO2

In general, sometimes an inexperienced practitioner can accidentally stick a vein instead of the artery when trying to obtain an ABG sample. When this occurs, the venous blood isn't oxygenated, so it has a darker appearance compared to the bright red arterial blood.

In this case, the best way to confirm that the sample is venous blood is to cross-check the results against the patient's SpO2. Because, when you run the results, the oxygenation values are going to be falsely low, again, since venous blood is not oxygenated.

You can check the patient's oxygen saturation with a pulse oximeter to see if it matches the results of the blood sample. Of course, if it is in fact venous blood, there won't be a match.

None of the other answer choices really make sense in this situation so we know that the correct answer has to be D.

The correct answer is: D. Cross-check the results against the patient's SpO2

29. A 176 lb male patient is intubated and receiving volume control A/C ventilation. His settings are as follows: 40% FiO2 at a rate of 12/min and a VT of 550 mL. A blood gas was drawn and bedside measurements displays the following results:

pH 7.39	Spontaneous VT 180 mL
PaCO2 37 mm Hg	Spontaneous Rate 37 breaths/min
HCO3 23 mEq/L	Vital Capacity 550 mL
PaO2 107 mm Hg	MIP/NIF -12 cm H2O

Which of the following actions would be appropriate at this time?

A. Place the patient on a 40% T-tube and monitor closely

B. Switch the patient to SIMV at a rate of 5/minute

C. Place the patient on 5 cm H2O CPAP and monitor closely

D. Maintain the current ventilator settings and re-evaluate later

To get this one right, you must be able to interpret the patient's ABG results and make the appropriate changes to the ventilator settings, or recommend the best course of action for the patient. These are the types of questions that you will see on the TMC Exam.

The first thing you should note is that the ABG results are all within the normal ranges. Then you can look at the bedside measurements.

The fast spontaneous rate, low spontaneous tidal volume, low vital capacity, and low MIP/NIF all indicate that the patient is not ready for a spontaneous breathing trial and should not yet be weaned. So in this case, you should maintain the current setting and re-evaluate the patient at a later time.

So since all of the other answer choices demonstrate a type of weaning, we know that the correct answer has to be D.

The correct answer is: D. Maintain the current ventilator settings and re-evaluate later

30. A 57-year-old female patient with emphysema has the following ABG results:
    pH 7.34
    PaCO2 65 torr
    PaO2 47 torr
    HCO3 31 mEq/L
    BE +6

    She is showing signs of shortness and has inspiratory crackles on auscultation. Which of the following would you recommend for this patient?
    A. Nonrebreathing mask at 10 L/min
    B. Air-entrainment mask at 28%
    C. Albuterol via a small-volume nebulizer
    D. Nasal cannula at 4 L/min

First you need to interpret the ABG results. The acid-base status shows that the patient is partially compensated respiratory acidosis. The other thing that should stand out is that the PaO2 is severely low, so you know that the patient needs supplemental oxygen.

For a patient with COPD, you must be careful not to give too much oxygen in order to avoid oxygen-induced hypercapnia. Remember, it's acceptable for COPD patients to have a PaO2 in the 55-70 torr range and an SpO2 in the 88 to 93% range.

There is no indication for a bronchodilator and a nonrebreather would provide too much oxygen for the patient. In this case, you need to be able to provide a precise low FiO2.

An air-entrainment mask can help you do just that. So with that said, we know that the correct answer has to be B.

The correct answer is: B. Air-entrainment mask at 28%

31. A 61-year-old male patient is post-abdominal surgery and has been on a high-flow nasal cannula at 20 L/min for three days. The patient's ABG results are as follows:
pH 7.39
PaCO2 43 torr
PaO2 157 torr
SaO2 99%
HCO3 24 mEq/L
BE +2

Which of the following is the best action to take at this time?
A. Decrease the flow
B. Decrease the FiO2
C. Decrease the flow and FiO2 together
D. Switch to standard nasal cannula

The first thing you need to do is interpret the ABG results. The acid-base status is normal because the pH, PaCO2, HCO3, and BE are all within the normal range.

However, the PaO2, on the other hand, is too high. So you know that you need to decrease this value, and you can do so by decreasing the FiO2.

In general for a high-flow nasal cannula, you need a flow of at least 20-30 L/min in order to deliver the set FiO2 to adult patients. So if you were to decrease the flow below 20 L/min, it's not going to provide the set FiO2.

And in general, you should avoid adjusting two parameters at the same time.

So by using our ABG interpretation skills, as well as what we know about high-flow nasal cannulas, you know that the correct answer has to be B.

The correct answer is: B. Decrease the FiO2

32. A 74 kg male patient intubated and receiving volume control A/C ventilation with the following settings: FiO2 of 50%, a set rate of 15, and a tidal volume of 550 mL. The patient's total respiratory rate is 29 breaths/min. His ABG results are as follows:
   pH 7.53
   PaCO2 27 torr
   HCO3 23 mEq/L
   BE -2
   PaO2 82 torr
   SaO2 97%
   Which of the following is the best action to take at this time?
   A. Increase the FiO2
   B. Increase the ventilator rate
   C. Increase the tidal volume
   D. Add mechanical deadspace

The first thing you should do is interpret the ABG results, which indicates that the patient has acute respiratory alkalosis. This means that the patient is hyperventilating and is blowing off too much CO2.

The PaO2 and SaO2 values are normal, so you do not need to increase the FiO2. The rate is already too fast, so you do not need to increase the rate. And by looking at the patient's body weight, you can see that the tidal volume is set appropriately at around 8 mL/kg.

This means that the best action is to add mechanical deadspace.

Adding mechanical deadspace to the circuit is a method for treating hyperventilation. It works because the patient will essentially rebreathe the gas from their anatomic deadspace, which will in turn, increase the PaCO2 levels.

So by breaking this question down and using our knowledge about ABG's and mechanical ventilation, we know that the correct answer has to be D.

The correct answer is: D. Add mechanical deadspace

33. A 58-year-old female is receiving volume control A/C ventilation at a rate of 12/min with a tidal volume of 450 mL and an FiO2 of 40%. Her ABG results are as follows:
pH 7.35
PaCO2 44 torr
HCO3 22 mEq/L
BE 0
PaO2 91 torr
SaO2 97%
Based on this information, you should recommend which of the following?
A. Decrease the minute ventilation
B. Discontinue mechanical ventilation
C. Administer IV bicarbonate
D. Maintain the current settings

The first thing you need to do is interpret the ABG results. By doing so, you will see that all of the values fall within the normal range. And by looking at the ventilator settings that it gives you in the question, everything appears to be set appropriately.

Therefore, no changes are indicated at this time. The settings should be left unchanged. So we know that the correct answer is D.

The correct answer is: D. Maintain the current settings

34. You are monitoring a stable patient that is receiving mechanical ventilation. His ABG results are as follows:
    pH 7.49
    PaCO2 29 mm Hg
    HCO3 24 mEq/L
    BE +1
    PaO2 87 mm Hg
    SaO2 96%
    Based on the results, which of the following actions should you take at this time?
    A. Add 10 cm H2O PEEP
    B. Increase the minute ventilation
    C. Decrease the tidal volume
    D. Maintain the current settings

To get this one right, you have to be able to interpret the ABG results and make the appropriate changes to the ventilator settings. These are the types of questions you will see on the TMC Exam. So let's break this one down.

The pH is increased which means alkalosis. The PaCO2 is decreased. The HCO3, BE, PaO2, and SaO2 are all within the normal range. This means that the patient has acute respiratory alkalosis.

In other words, the patient is hyperventilating.

When a patient is hyperventilating, or breathing too fast, you need to decrease the minute ventilation. You can do that by either decreasing the rate or decreasing the tidal volume.

By looking at the answer choices, only one of the two is listed, so we know that the correct answer has to be C.

The correct answer is: C. Decrease the tidal volume

35. A patient is intubated and is receiving mechanical ventilation on the pressure control A/C mode at a rate of 10/min and peak pressure of 35 cm H2O. Her ABG results are as follows:
   pH 7.31
   PaCO2 49 torr
   SaO2 96%
   HCO3 23 mEq/L
   BE -2 mEq/L
   Which of the following actions should you take at this time?
   A. Increase the FiO2
   B. Increase the rate
   C. Change the patient to CPAP
   D. Make no changes at this time

First and foremost, we have to interpret the ABG results. The pH is low. The PaCO2 is high. The SaO2, HCO3, and BE are all within the normal range. This tells us that the patient has acute respiratory acidosis with normal oxygenation.

This means that the patient is hypoventilating, which is what is causing the increased PaCO2. So in order to blow over some of that CO2, you simply need to increase the rate. The correct answer has to be B.

The correct answer is: B. Increase the rate

Section 2
(Test Mode)

1. An adult patient with shortness of breath is admitted to the emergency department. An ABG has been collected and shows the following results:
   pH 7.51
   PaCO2 26 torr
   PaO2 57 torr
   HCO3- 24 mEq/L
   Which of the following best describes the patient's status?
   A. The patient has a metabolic issue
   B. The patient is hypoventilating
   C. The primary concern is hypoxemia
   D. The patient is in impending respiratory failure

2. The physician put in an order for an ABG that was not STAT. You weren't busy so you went ahead and collected the sample. What is the best way to avoid analysis errors associated with running the sample?
    A. Analyze the sample immediately
    B. Place the sample in an ice slush
    C. Use dry instead or liquid heparin
    D. Uncap the syringe to remove any air

3. The physician ordered an ABG on a 41-year-old patient with COPD. Before drawing the sample from the radial artery, which of the following should be performed?
   A. Check the patient's oxygen saturation
   B. Modified Allen test
   C. Nail bed blanching
   D. Blood pressure measurement

4. A 48-year-old female patient has been admitted to the emergency department with the following arterial blood gas results:
   pH 7.54
   PaCO2 29 torr
   PaO2 86 torr
   HCO3- 24 mEq/L
   Which of the following is the best interpretation of these results?
   A. Metabolic acidosis
   B. Metabolic alkalosis
   C. Respiratory acidosis
   D. Respiratory alkalosis

5. You are needed to help with the treatment of a patient with pneumonia that is receiving oxygen via nasal cannula at 4 L/min. The physician asks for your suggestion of the best way to evaluate the patient's overall ability to breathe. What should you recommend?
    A. Performing pulse oximetry
    B. Drawing an arterial blood sample for analysis
    C. Performing a forced vital capacity measurement
    D. Doing a full set of pulmonary function tests

6. A 56-year-old male patient's status has gotten worse over the past 2 hours. He went from an air entrainment mask to a nonrebreather, and is now receiving positive pressure ventilation with the following settings:
   Assist control rate of 12
   Tidal volume 650 mL
   FIO2 100%
   PIP 40 cm H2O
   Plateau pressure 35 cm H2
The patient's arterial blood gas results are:
   pH 7.42
   PaCO2 35 torr
   PaO2 54 torr
   SpO2 84%
   HCO3- 23 mEq/L
Which of the following best represents the status of this patient?
   A. Cystic fibrosis
   B. Acute metabolic alkalosis
   C. Hypoventilation from fatigue
   D. A significant intrapulmonary shunt

7. A 60-year-old female patient has been admitted to the emergency department with the following ABG results:
   pH 7.48
   PaCO2 41 torr
   PaO2 98 torr
   HCO3- 52 mEq/L
   These results of this ABG can be interpreted as:
   A. Respiratory alkalosis
   B. Respiratory acidosis
   C. Metabolic alkalosis
   D. Metabolic acidosis

8. An ABG is drawn on 71-year-old patient with a history of chronic COPD. After reviewing the patient's ABG results, which of the following values would be most reflective of the severity of the patient's chronic condition?
   A. pH
   B. PaCO2
   C. HCO3-
   D. PaO2

9. A patient has been admitted to the emergency department with the following arterial blood gas results:
   pH 7.24
   PaCO2 29 torr
   PaO2 81 torr
   HCO3- 13 mEq/L
   Which of the following best describes the given results?
   D. Partially compensated metabolic alkalosis
   B. Partially compensated metabolic acidosis
   C. Uncompensated respiratory acidosis
   A. Uncompensated respiratory alkalosis

10. The following ABG results were obtained on a 54-year-old female patient that is breathing room air:
    pH 7.30
    PaCO2 57 torr
    PaO2 61 torr
    HCO3- 24 mEq/L
    Which of the following best describes the given results?
    A. Normal blood gas with mild hypoxemia
    B. Fully compensated metabolic acidosis with mild hypoxemia
    C. Acute respiratory alkalosis with mild hypoxemia
    D. Acute uncompensated respiratory acidosis with mild hypoxemia

11. A patient with acute respiratory acidosis would be expected to have a base excess in the range of which of the following?
    A. + 6 mEq/L
    B. - 6 mEq/L
    C. +/- 2 mEq/L
    D. +/- 8 mEq/L

12. Which of the following ABG results would you most likely see for a patient who is having a mild asthma attack?
    A. pH = 7.30 PaCO2 = 49 torr PaO2 = 61 torr
    B. pH = 7.41 PaCO2 = 51 torr PaO2 = 51 torr
    C. pH = 7.45 PaCO2 = 42 torr PaO2 = 52 torr
    D. pH = 7.47 PaCO2 = 30 torr PaO2 = 62 torr

13. The following ABG results were obtained on a 28-year-old female patient:
    pH 7.28
    PaCO2 22 torr
    HCO3 12 mEq/L
    BE -13
    PaO2 111 torr
    Her ABG results indicate which of the following?
    A. Acute metabolic alkalosis
    B. Partially compensated metabolic acidosis
    C. Partially compensated respiratory alkalosis
    D. Acute respiratory acidosis

14. A 61-year-old female patient with a history of COPD was admitted to the emergency department for an acute case suspected pneumonia. Her ABG results are as follows:
    pH = 7.19
    PCO2 = 66 torr
    HCO3 = 26 mEq/L
    PaO2 = 41 torr
    P(A-a)O2 = 43 torr
    Which of the following best describes the patient's condition?
    A. Acute hypercapnic respiratory failure
    B. Chronic hypercapnic respiratory failure
    C. Acute hypoxemic respiratory failure
    D. Combined hypercapnic and hypoxemic respiratory failure

15. A 48-year-old male patient is receiving volume-control SIMV with 40% oxygen and has following ABG results:
    pH 7.51
    PaCO2 27 torr
    PaO2 85 torr
    HCO3 24 mEq/L
    BE -1

    The patient's blood gas results indicate which of the following?
    A. Acute respiratory alkalosis
    B. Acute respiratory acidosis
    C. Acute metabolic alkalosis
    D. Acute hypoxemic failure

16. Which of the following problems is most likely associated with a patient whose ABG results show respiratory alkalosis?
    A. Hypoxemia
    B. Hypothermia
    C. CNS depression
    D. Opiate overdose

17. A 54-year-old female patient on the general floor has the following ABG results:
    pH = 7.53
    pCO2 = 44 torr
    HCO3 = 34 mEq/L
    Which of the following is the best interpretation of these results?
    A. Acute respiratory alkalosis
    B. Acute metabolic alkalosis
    C. Compensated respiratory alkalosis
    D. Combined respiratory and metabolic alkalosis

18. While interpreting a patient's ABG results, you note a PaCO2 of 24 torr, a Base Excess of -11 mEq/L, and a pH of 7.36. How would you interpret these results?
   A. Acute respiratory alkalosis
   B. Acute metabolic acidosis
   C. Compensated respiratory alkalosis
   D. Compensated metabolic acidosis

19. A 69-year-old male patient in the ICU displays the following ABG results:
    pH = 7.43
    pCO2 = 21 torr
    HCO3 = 13 mEq/L
    His ABG results can be interpreted as which of the following?
    A. Acute respiratory alkalosis
    B. Partially compensated respiratory alkalosis
    C. Fully compensated respiratory alkalosis
    D. Combined respiratory and metabolic alkalosis

20. A patient's ABG results show that she has a pH of 7.56 and a PaCO2 of 48 torr. Based on the results given, how would you interpret the patient's status?
    A. Respiratory alkalosis
    B. Respiratory acidosis
    C. Metabolic acidosis
    D. Metabolic alkalosis

21. You were just called by the physician for a STAT ABG. Before entering the patient's room, you must first gather all the necessary supplies. Which of the following is required in order to perform an arterial puncture?
    A. Sterile gloves
    B. Lancet
    C. Local anesthetic
    D. Anticoagulant

22. There is an order to obtain a blood sample from a neonate. It is determined that you should obtain the sample from a capillary instead of the artery. Which of the following is true regarding a capillary blood gas sample?

   A. To obtain the sample, you need to milk the puncture site
   B. The sample must be drawn from the first drop of surface blood
   C. The pH and PCO2 correlate well with arterial blood
   D. The puncture normally is performed on the ball of the foot

23. Which of the following infection control procedures is to be used when drawing an arterial blood gas?
    A. Hand washing and gloves only
    B. Gown and protective eyewear
    C. Mask and protective eyewear
    D. All CDC standard precautions

24. After collecting an ABG sample, you are about the analyze the sample using a point-of-care analyzer. During the process, the device flags the PaCO2 results. Which of the following should you do at this time?
A. Send the sample to the central lab for analysis
B. Repeat the analysis using a fresh sample and the same cartridge
C. Repeat analysis using a fresh sample and new cartridge
D. Repeat the analysis using the same sample and same cartridge

25. A patient in the emergency department is receiving oxygen via a nonrebreather at 15 L/min. There ABG results are as follows:
    pH 7.21
    PaCO2 38 torr
    PaO2 569 torr
    SpO2 100%
    HCO3 23 mEq/L
    BE -1
    Which of the following is the best interpretation for these results?
    A. Respiratory acidosis
    B. Metabolic acidosis
    C. Laboratory error
    D. Large physiologic shunt

26. A 51-year-old patient on room air has the following ABG results:
    pH 7.43
    PaCO2 47 torr
    PaO2 169 torr
    Which of the following is the best action to take?
    A. Report the results to the attending physician
    B. Report the results to the patient's nurse
    C. Discard the sample and obtain a new one
    D. Give the patient a bronchodilator treatment

27. A patient with a flail chest arrives to the emergency department and is hyperventilating. Which of the following ABG results would you expect to find for this patient?
    A. Increased pH and decreased SaO2
    B. Increased pH and increased SaO2
    C. Decreased pH and decreased SaO2
    D. Decreased pH and increased SaO2

28. After drawing an ABG sample, you notice that the blood appears to be darker in color. You suspect that obtained sample is actually venous blood. Which of the following would be the best way to confirm this suspicion?
    A. Get a second opinion from the attending physician
    B. Compute the alveolar-arterial O2 gradient
    C. Compute the patient's P/F ratio
    D. Cross-check the results against the patient's SpO2

29. A 176 lb male patient is intubated and receiving volume control A/C ventilation. His settings are as follows: 40% FiO2 at a rate of 12/min and a VT of 550 mL. A blood gas was drawn and bedside measurements displays the following results:

pH 7.39	Spontaneous VT 180 mL
PaCO2 37 mm Hg	Spontaneous Rate 37 breaths/min
HCO3 23 mEq/L	Vital Capacity 550 mL
PaO2 107 mm Hg	MIP/NIF -12 cm H2O

Which of the following actions would be appropriate at this time?

A. Place the patient on a 40% T-tube and monitor closely

B. Switch the patient to SIMV at a rate of 5/minute

C. Place the patient on 5 cm H2O CPAP and monitor closely

D. Maintain the current ventilator settings and re-evaluate later

30. A 57-year-old female patient with emphysema has the following ABG results:
    pH 7.34
    PaCO2 65 torr
    PaO2 47 torr
    HCO3 31 mEq/L
    BE +6

    She is showing signs of shortness and has inspiratory crackles on auscultation. Which of the following would you recommend for this patient?
    A. Nonrebreathing mask at 10 L/min
    B. Air-entrainment mask at 28%
    C. Albuterol via a small-volume nebulizer
    D. Nasal cannula at 4 L/min

31. A 61-year-old male patient is post-abdominal surgery and has been on a high-flow nasal cannula at 20 L/min for three days. The patient's ABG results are as follows:
pH 7.39
PaCO2 43 torr
PaO2 157 torr
SaO2 99%
HCO3 24 mEq/L
BE +2
Which of the following is the best action to take at this time?
A. Decrease the flow
B. Decrease the FiO2
C. Decrease the flow and FiO2 together
D. Switch to standard nasal cannula

32. A 74 kg male patient intubated and receiving volume control A/C ventilation with the following settings: FiO2 of 50%, a set rate of 15, and a tidal volume of 550 mL. The patient's total respiratory rate is 29 breaths/min. His ABG results are as follows:
   pH 7.53
   PaCO2 27 torr
   HCO3 23 mEq/L
   BE -2
   PaO2 82 torr
   SaO2 97%
   Which of the following is the best action to take at this time?
   A. Increase the FiO2
   B. Increase the ventilator rate
   C. Increase the tidal volume
   D. Add mechanical deadspace

33. A 58-year-old female is receiving volume control A/C ventilation at a rate of 12/min with a tidal volume of 450 mL and an FiO2 of 40%. Her ABG results are as follows:
pH 7.35
PaCO2 44 torr
HCO3 22 mEq/L
BE 0
PaO2 91 torr
SaO2 97%
Based on this information, you should recommend which of the following?
A. Decrease the minute ventilation
B. Discontinue mechanical ventilation
C. Administer IV bicarbonate
D. Maintain the current settings

34. You are monitoring a stable patient that is receiving mechanical ventilation. His ABG results are as follows:
    pH 7.49
    PaCO2 29 mm Hg
    HCO3 24 mEq/L
    BE +1
    PaO2 87 mm Hg
    SaO2 96%
    Based on the results, which of the following actions should you take at this time?
    A. Add 10 cm H2O PEEP
    B. Increase the minute ventilation
    C. Decrease the tidal volume
    D. Maintain the current settings

35. A patient is intubated and is receiving mechanical ventilation on the pressure control A/C mode at a rate of 10/min and peak pressure of 35 cm H2O. Her ABG results are as follows:
pH 7.31
PaCO2 49 torr
SaO2 96%
HCO3 23 mEq/L
BE -2 mEq/L
Which of the following actions should you take at this time?
A. Increase the FiO2
B. Increase the rate
C. Change the patient to CPAP
D. Make no changes at this time

Conclusion

And that wraps up our practice questions on Arterial Blood Gases. I truly hope these questions can help you study and learn the information necessary for you to ace the TMC Exam when that time comes.

People often ask me, "What's the easiest way to pass the TMC Exam on my first try?" I always give the same exact answer:

You practice.

It's that simple. You've already spent months in the classroom learning everything you need to know. Now you just need to put it all together and you can do that by practicing with real-life practice questions exactly like the ones you'll see on the real thing.

If you liked the practice questions in this book and found them to be helpful, I have good news. This is only a small sample of what we have for our students.

You can check out our **TMC Test Bank**, which is loaded with tons of practice questions and explanations, just like the ones here in this book.

The good thing is, we cover each and every topic that you must know for the exam, including more questions on Arterial Blood Gases.

To get exclusive access to over 1000 practice questions, just go to:

RespiratoryTherapyZone.com/tmc

Our valued customers always get a discount. Just use the coupon code **thankyou** at checkout.

Thank you so much for reading this book. I wish you the best of luck as you study and prepare for the exam. Keep studying and working hard and I know you'll be successful when you take the exam and start your career as a Respiratory Therapist.

And as always, breathe easy my friend!

If you liked this book, please consider leaving a 5-star review on Amazon. Thank you very much!

One more thing!

How would you like to get new TMC Practice Questions sent to your inbox every single day?

If this is something that sounds interesting to you, definitely consider signing up for our **Practice Questions Pro Membership**.

It literally costs pennies on the dollar compared to the value that you receive.

To learn more, go to:

RespiratoryTherapyZone.com/pro

Breathe easy, my friend!

References

1. AARC Clinical Practice Guidelines, (2002-2019) Respirator Care. www.aarc.org.

2. Egan's Fundamentals of Respiratory Care. (2010) 11th Edition. Kacmarek, RM, Stoller, JK, Heur, AH. Elsevier.

3. Mosby's Respiratory Care Equipment. Cairo, JM. (2014) 9th Edition. Elsevier.

4. Pilbeam's Mechanical Ventilation. (2012) Cairo, JM. Physiological and Clinical Applications. 5th Edition. Saunders, Elsevier.

5. Ruppel's Manual of Pulmonary Function Testing. (2013) Mottram, C. 10th Edition. Elsevier.

6. Rau's Respiratory Care Pharmacology. (2012) Gardenhire, DS. 8th Edition. Elsevier.

7. Perinatal and Pediatric Respiratory Care. (2010) Walsh, BK, Czervinske, MP, DiBlasi, RM. 3rd Edition. Saunders.

8. Wilkins' Clinical Assessment in Respiratory Care (2013) Heuer, Al. 7th Edition. Saunders. Elsevier.

9. Clinical Manifestations and Assessment of Respiratory Disease. (2010) Des Jardins, T, & Burton, GG. 6th edition. Elsevier.

10. Neonatal and Pediatric Respiratory Care. (2014) Walsh, Brian K. 4th edition. RRT. Elsevier.

11. Clinical Application of Mechanical Ventilation (2013) Chang, David W. 4th edition. Cengage Learning.

Copyright © Respiratory Therapy Zone

Made in the USA
Monee, IL
03 December 2021

83827907R00055